God's Little Artist

"Ma religion et mon art, c'est toute ma vie"
— *Gwen John*

God's Little Artist

Sue Hubbard

SEREN

Seren is the book imprint of
Poetry Wales Press Ltd.
Suite 6, 4 Derwen Road, Bridgend, Wales, CF31 1LH
www.serenbooks.com
facebook.com/SerenBooks
twitter@SerenBooks

www.serenbooks.com
facebook.com/SerenBooks
twitter@SerenBooks

The right of Sue Hubbard to be identified as
the author of this work has been asserted in accordance
with the Copyright, Designs and Patents Act, 1988.

© Sue Hubbard, 2023.

ISBN: 978-1-78172-716-4

A CIP record for this title is available from the British Library.

The publisher acknowledges the financial assistance of the Books Council of Wales.

Cover painting: Gwen John, *The Convalescent*, 1915-1925

Contents

Introduction

'When I was a child,' Gwen John said in middle-age to a friend, 'I used to cry all the time, and they told me, "don't cry now, when you're grown up, you'll have something to cry about." So I was afraid of growing up and I never expected any happiness in life.' Born in 1876 in Haverfordwest, Wales, Gwen John's father, Edwin, was a solicitor and her sociable mother, Augusta, liked to play Chopin on the piano and paint in watercolours. A sufferer from chronic rheumatism, she was rarely well and, for much of Gwen's childhood, was away from home seeking cures. After her sudden death, when Gwen was eight, Edwin moved his four children (including Gwen's precociously talented brother Augustus) to Tenby. There they were educated by a series of governesses, running wild on Tenby's wide beach, playing in the sand without socks or shoes, to the consternation of their conservative neighbours. Later Gwen would leave Wales to study at the Slade and spend much of the rest of her life in Paris. There she would fall under the spell of the celebrated and much older sculptor Rodin, with whom she had an anguished relationship.

In his seminal work, *Attachment and Loss*, the psychoanalyst John Bowlby concludes that the loss of the mother — whether through death, illness, or emotional unavailability at an early age — has a devastating effect on a child's mental well-being. The mother's role in the child's formative years is to provide a secure emotional base to which they can return safely during their initial explorations of the world. If the mother figure is removed, the infant may go through a sequence of emotions from angry protest, lethargic despair to detachment. A child who is certain that its attachment figures are available when needed will usually develop a sense of security and inner confidence that forms the template for their more mature relationships. While the bereaved or abandoned child might continue to search for that lost maternal succour by clinging to other, often inappropriate, relationships and be vulnerable to depression and anxiety when those relationships are withdrawn. Rilke, Trollope, Edward Lear, Rudyard Kipling, P.G. Woodhouse, Munch and Degas — to name just a few — are writers and artists who all suffered degrees of maternal deprivation and used their creative imaginations to give meaning and structure to their lives. As Georges Simenon claimed in an interview for Paris Review in 1958: 'Writing is not a profession but a vocation of unhappiness'. The same might be said of art.

Those who possess major artistic talent are often thought of as peculiar or eccentric. In his book on *Solitude*, the psychiatrist Anthony Storr, suggests that what goes on in the mind of an individual when they are alone – the imaginative process – is as fundamentally important as the creation of interpersonal connections. Quoting the influential paediatrician and psychoanalyst Donald Winnicott, Storr recounts 'The capacity to be alone thus becomes linked with self-discovery and self-realisation; with becoming aware of one's deepest needs, feelings and impulses.' Gwen John spent a good deal of time alone. To be an independent female artist at the end of the 19th century and the beginning of the 20th was a near impossibility. She had originally come to Paris with the bohemian Dorelia, her brother Augustus's mistress, whom she had met at the Slade. Montparnasse, where she lived, was full of little bars, junk shops and artists' studios. Second-hand book stalls lined the banks of the Seine and on every corner there was a flower seller where, for a few centimes, you could buy a bunch of fragrant narcissi. For two years Gwen lodged in the Hôtel Mont Blanc. By modelling for other artists she was able to pay for her meagre furnished room. The streets outside were busy, grimy and smelly. A stink of open drains and *pommes frites* wafted in through her windows. Rilke, who was in Paris from 1902 to spring 1903, thought the area smelt of fear. Money was always a problem. In order to paint, Gwen, and her near contemporary the German Expressionist artist Paula Modersohn-Becker who was in Paris around the same time, lived close to the poverty line. For a young female artist without means life was almost untenable. Today we may romanticise the artist's attic, but such a frugal existence lived out at the top of a damp building with insufficient coal and not enough to eat, without running water, electricity or plumbing was, to put it mildly, taxing. Such a way of life needed huge inner resources.

After Dorelia announced her return to Augustus to live in a *menage à trois* with his wife, Ida Nettleship, in a gypsy caravan, Gwen met Rodin. It was 1904. She knocked on his studio door and asked if she could model for him. He was the most famous artist of the age and thirty-six years her senior. Initially he was entranced by this intense little Welsh girl. She loved to pose for him, to talk about literature and the work of other artists but soon she became obsessed, sending him a never-ending stream of letters, waiting for hours in her little room for him to visit.

In their 1978 study of depression among working class women, *Social Origins of Depression*, George Brown and Tirril Harris concluded that, if a woman experienced the death of her mother before the age of eleven, she was more likely to respond to subsequent rejections and losses by developing severe depression. Women who had experienced childhood bereavement showed greater difficulty in achieving mature, adult attachments. The relationship with Rodin, where his art was always his primary concern, heightened both Gwen's visual and sexual awareness, making her all the more needy and dependent. She wanted to be with him all the time. To stop working. To be absorbed by his great presence. And, of course, the more she wanted him, the more he backed away. Alone in her room at night, she wrote a stream of yearning letters expressing her longing for what was impossible, to be always with him, to be his whole world, though he lived in Meudon with his long term companion, Rose Beuret, a onetime seamstress and laundress, whom he married just weeks before her death, in 1917.

In 1906 Gwen moved to a new room in the rue St. Placide and continued to write to him and study the books on philosophy he gave her. But whatever she did, it never felt enough. For a while she even stopped painting but, slowly, her new room brought her back to herself and to her art. It was here that she began a series of haunting self-portraits and studies of women. It was as if, through these small works, she might discover who she really was, find her place in the world. Bathed in soft evening light, paintings such as *La Chambre sur la Cour*, are full of beatific harmonies borrowed from Renaissance painting and the tonalites of Pierro della Francesca. The idea for such works may well have been prompted by her talks with Rilke who was, at the time, sharing his own thoughts on solitude with the young poet Franz Xaver Kappus, later to be published as *Letters to a Young Poet*:

> And you should not let yourself be confused in your solitude by the fact that there is something in you that wants to move out of it. This very wish, if you used it calmly and prudently and like a tool, will help you spread out your solitude over a great distance. Most people have conventionally turned their solutions towards what is easy and towards the easiest side of the easy, but we must insist on what is difficult;.....We know little, but that we must trust in difficulty is a certainty that will never abandon us; it is good to be solitary, for solitude is difficult; and something that is difficult must be one reason for us to do it.....

After her affair with Rodin finally drew to a close Gwen John sought comfort in Catholicism, spending the rest of her life in near seclusion. She visited the Mother Superior of a nearby convent who encouraged her in Catholic instruction and she was commissioned to paint Mère Marie Poussepin, the 17th century founder of the order. Around this time she wrote in her notebook, 'Rules to Keep the World Away.' There were ten that included 'Do not listen to people (more than is necessary)....Do not look at people....have as little intercourse with people as possible....talk as little as possible....do not look in shop windows....Do not care for the opinion of people – or work for it in any way.' She resolved to be alone, not to 'search for sympathy where it is not to be found. '

In her famous statement *ma religion et mon art c'est toute ma vie*, it might be argued that Gwen replaced her obsession for Rodin with one for God, one that allowed her an emotionally secure place from which to paint. In 1939, after the death of her father, she made her will in Meudon, then travelled to Dieppe, taking no luggage, where she collapsed and died.

Something of a myth has grown up since her death, that of a reclusive, solitary person who neglected her health and rejected the world. To modern sensibilities Gwen John's behaviour seems eccentric. In a society dominated by social media, where we're connected to incessant meaningless chatter, to be quiet and turn away into solitude is considered aberrant. Yet Anthony Storr suggests that for many gifted people who, for some reason or another do not have close personal relationships, creativity can be every bit as significant and meaningful. The American poet Elizabeth Bishop believed that everyone should experience at least one extensive period of solitude in life. Being alone is different from being lonely. It is the mulch from which our deepest creative endeavours spring. It is in solitude that many artists, thinkers and writers have made their best work. Recent studies have found that while people thrive on being sociable, it is when they are alone for prolonged periods that they are at their most creative. The well of solitude deliberately plumbed by Gwen John gave rise to a series of paintings that in their subtle tonalities and still, meditative quality are among the most potent produced at the turn of the last century. 'Do not have many little aims,' she wrote, 'but one great one – to be a child of prayer and God's artist.'

Luncheon in Tenby

The mahogany sideboard reclines
against the wall like the chief mourner
at a funeral. Bow-windows
hang heavy with dark velvet drapes.

On the marble mantle the skeleton
clock ticks endless seconds
into the stillness. The rice-pudding's
glutinous lumps are making her gag.

Her father demands quiet, so she
and Winifred speak in signs. From
the basement they hear Mrs Mackenzie
singing *Bread of Heaven* with the kitchen maid,

their skylark voices rising in
the mortuary hush, the stuffed doves
beneath their glass dome
condemned to perpetual silence.

Naked

The promenade will no longer do.
She yearns for Lydstep's wild

and windy beach, its palisade of cliffs
and smugglers' cave, the blowhole

that sends up plumes of dolphin spray
into the field above. The grit of sand

between her toes. Bathing naked
off the rocks where she swims too far out,

invigorated by the thought
she might not get back again.

But today the school crocodile's
marching along the strand,

damp donkeys huddled
in the spitting spray,

while, up ahead, Augustus is pulling off
his clothes, flinging them pell-mell

across the rocks, cavorting in the buff
in front of his red-faced master.

Slade

She takes the train to London—
leaving her stern father
with his taxidermy and law tomes,
his shelves of devotional works—
to embrace anatomy, perspective,
and the history of art,
to gather in cheap cafes smelling
of stewed tea and stale buns
on the Euston Road,
visit the theatre in Drury Lane,
with other fresh-faced girls
cramped in a shilling box.
At work in the life-room
from ten till five,
she learns from Tonks
a new freedom of line.
How to evoke round objects
on flat paper. Three dimensions
whilst working in two.
Describe light falling on
cloth and skin, breathe life
into an old mackintosh,
a coffee spoon.

Glaze

Crossing the quadrangle she climbs
the honey-coloured steps,
passing though the Corinthian columns.

To the right is the Women's studio
but, being new, she's banished
to the Antique Room

in the basement for a year
with sheets of Ingres paper,
a stub of tomato-coloured chalk

to draw Discobolus and Venus de Milo
(in the classical manner)
before admission to the Life Room.

Even then, the women are strictly
segregated, the male nudes never
completely nude. Tonks keeps

a skeleton in his cupboard,
insisting that only when they know
how the femur rotates in the pelvic socket,

the radius hinges on the ulna,
will they be able to draw from life.
Everything inside her rebels.

She's not a surgeon, won't
make maps of sinew and bone
in ochre, black and white,

but longs to experiment with glazes
luminous as veils of sea-haze
hanging over her Tenby cliffs,

that soft and sudden light
like a line of graphite shimmering
between sea and Welsh sky.

Walking with Dorelia

They take the Thames steamer
to Bordeaux, then the road

to Toulouse, intending to go to Rome,
sleeping under haystacks and icy stars,

lying on top of each other to stay warm.
They wake to astonished farmers,

gathered gendarmes peering curiously
at *les jeunes Anglaises déshaibillées*

huddled under a pagoda of portfolios,
straw woven in their tangled hair.

Surviving on bread and grapes,
on beer, they become lightheaded

with sleeplessness and hunger.
Laden with canvases, smeared with dust,

they arrive like moths in village twilight,
sketch café patrons to earn their keep.

Sing, if they must, for their supper.
In her flamboyant petticoats Dorelia

is all gypsy. Her slim throat white
as the swan goddess' who appeared

to Aengus on Lough Muskry
in all her frightful beauty.

Montmartre

She wakes to luminous striations
    seeping through the shutters
like something holy.
    Sun pools on the scrubbed

deal floor, the chipped lip
    of her blue china jug.
A rosary of sounds floats through
    her high window across

chimney pots and rooftops,
    the croo of pigeons and clanging trams,
cats fighting for fishbones in the gutter.
    Below, carthorses stamp and steam

amid the mire. On the street corner,
    crippled in her sooty blacks,
la petite fleuriste hawks bunches
    of *muguet* and yellow mimosa.

Across Sunday streets
    bells drift above junk shops
and cheap bars where *des maudits*
    nurse glasses of cloudy absinthe.

Far from Tenby
    this, now, is home.
To eat, she knocks on studio doors,
    poses, if she can, for women.

The men are rude.
    Ask her to undress, place
insolent hands on her small breasts
    to check she's *développée*.

Their breath acrid as the morning
    blood between her thighs,
though she's too proud to tell them
    as she turns to leave, *I paint*.

Modelling for Rodin

Naked before him,
she finds a new peace,

feels pleasure in her nudity.
All day she longs for the moment

his assistants are dismissed,
when he will light the bees-wax candles

in their bottles – preferring their gentle
hues to the flat brightness of gas jets –

as he stalks the dimming studio
to examine his work.

Stock-still, she will wait
until he stands before her,

reaching for her small breasts.
Then the weight of him,

his tongue in her mouth
like something feral.

Oh mon Maître

She lies beneath peeling plaster,
stars hanging like silver apples

outside her attic window.
There's nothing to be done.

For love cannot be bought
like a kilo of plums.

Across the city he sleeps
in a separate bed,

chest rising and falling
beneath his grizzled beard.

The bodies of other women,
legs splayed pleasuring themselves,

fill the sketchbook
beneath his shuttered eyelids.

Loneliness has always been her story.
In the Bon Marché she buys

lace-edged chemises,
silk stockings to tempt him

but at sixty-three, he's easily tired.
Dappled in moonlight,

her slight body lies sprawled
across the iron bed, her cotton shift

rucked about her thighs, her skin
cold as alabaster in the night air.

Love is lonelier than solitude

She thinks of him all the time,
an anchorite in her quiet cell
waiting for his booted step on the stair,

reluctant to go out in case he comes.
All is clean and polished. Her hair washed,
bluebells in a jar on the mantle,

a bow around Tiger's neck.
He complains she gives him headaches,
interferes with his work.

Then when the light begins to fade
she buttons up her shift, accompanies him
to the station to board the train for Meudon

where Rose is picking peas
in the evening garden. Rose will feed him,
wash his clothes, but these drawings

they make together are their children.
These charcoal smears, her puckered skin.
This. They will always have this.

Fire

He won't be alone with her now.
Tells her that her little room
with its pretty wallpaper
in stripes and criss-cross pattern,

is too hot and humid.
She's afraid it's an excuse,
that the flame-haired American
who's replacing his tobacco tweeds,

his black felt hat with tailcoats
and seal-skin toppers, dancing for him
to the wind-up gramophone,
is putting Red Indian love potions in his milk.

At night she cannot sleep.
Her sheets still smell of him.
Sweat. Turps. Semen.
Outside her high window cold stars

hang among the sooty flues.
Oh, that she could reach out
and pluck them from the velvet night,
bind him to her wrought-iron bed

with their jagged points.
Tie his wrists with stockings
of moonlight, straddle him
till she catches fire.

Hands

Her floral print dress lies crushed
like scattered violets on the studio floor.

From behind the cupboard door
the cross-eyed concierge watches

as he takes her again and again.
Sometimes his Finnish assistant–

the one who thinks she's ugly–
sits hidden in the corner to catch

a glimpse of bare buttock,
the rosy bud of a nipple.

Occasionally they invite her
to join in.

On days he refuses them both
they draw each other,

lie together on the big brass bed, .
their flesh dissolving

in tsunamis of delight,
as they touch again and again,

imagining his beard, his meaty hands,
the weight of his barrel chest.

Drawing the cat

Rodin insists she must draw every day,
though she wants only to button his boots,

brush his coat and light his stove,
smooth down his dear hair.

Longing to make him proud,
she picks up the pencils he gave her,

begins to draw the cat,
though she's not an easy model.

With her head coquettishly turned,
she's half-girl, half-beast,

indolently waiting
for those thick fingers to knead

her brindled fur, her undulating muscles,
the sinuous curve of her back.

Letter to Rodin

After a long day modelling
she stops for bread
in the rue Cherche Midi,
a single slice of ham
from the *charcuterie* in St Placide,
then tiptoes up the narrow stairs
to avoid the eye
of the mountainous concierge.
Tiger is waiting,
but she doesn't light the stove
or lamp. Let's her tea grow cold.
Forgets to eat.
Raindrops slither down
the skylight's milky glass.
A flood of moonshine spills
onto the round table,
the blank white sheet,
a millrace of words pulling
her under, soaking her wet.

Suitors

Women like her, too–
though she keeps herself to herself–
particularly the fat one
she passes daily in the rue St. Placide.

When they meet in the *crémerie,*
she stands too close, rubbing herself,
lascivious as a street cat, against
the white-tiled wall beside the milk churns,

to expose her ample calves beneath
the hem of her filthy skirt.
Then there's the Russian painter
who comes to the studio bearing

croissants and cream puffs,
wanting her to go to the music hall.
The Gaieté in Montparnasse where
plump-bellied chorus girls shock

the audience with their wiggling.
But when she tries to sneak a kiss,
Gwen moves away; her breath
stinks, and she's a terrible painter.

The Poetry of Things

She prefers to draw in the clean light
of morning, dissecting her naked

reflection in the foxed glass.
But if the weather's fine she takes

her sketchbook to copy the concierge's
old tabby cat, the pair of dray horses

stamping by the café's red door,
(though she has trouble with the ears).

There is poetry in ordinary things,
her blue jug, the basket of kittens,

that line of busy ants.
In the Jardin de Luxembourg

clouds of spray form droplets
on the Verdigris fountain,

strings of prayer beads
lucent as benedictions.

Communion

The stove won't work. She's got a bad cough.
Her nights are as long as the strung-out days.

Drawing calms her nerves, so she takes her notebook
to Gare Montparnasse, sketches travellers with carpet bags

and furled umbrellas, though her chilblained fingers are freezing.
She speaks to no one. Loneliness seeps beneath

her thin chemise pungent as sweat in the station din.
At home there's only the heavy tread of her unseen

neighbour on the stair, never the steps she longs for.
To punish him she won't eat. Is disgusted by the smell of food,

boils chestnuts in sugar milk not to contaminate her room,
convinced that meals in cafés are poisoned.

Waking each morning with migraines, *la grippe*, she knows
she must let go, that passion cannot be caged like a yellow canary.

Lying at night in her narrow bed, pilgrim hands clasped across
her scrawny breasts, she surrenders to the dark, to its silent order.

Life Drawing

She loves the consolation of the Mass,
its candles and smell of incense,

the evening shadows spilling
across the cold stone floor

through a sieve of coloured light.
Rows of kneeling school girls

in black dresses, heads bowed
before their *prie-dieux*.

The white ribbons
of their broad-brimmed hats

streaked against the growing dark.
She pulls out a pencil,

begins with a thick plait
snaking down a bony back,

the nuns' winged headdresses
big as dinner plates.

In the hush of her attic room
the night absorbs all colour,

casting veils of chalky white,
of ivory and black.

Tired now, wrung out,
she's almost transparent.

Attic

A mother-of-pearl light
seeps through the voile curtains.

Roof tops hang scribbled
against the bleached Parisian sky.

On the altar of her deal table
a single jar of apple blossom

sits like a bridal bouquet.
Everything immaculate

for her spring-cleaned soul.
Beneath the yellow-papered eave

her wicker chair kneels in meditation,
her white umbrella hooked

by the crook of its long neck,
bows in penitent prayer.

Over its willow arm
her crumpled shawl hangs

in a cloud of indigo grief.
She parts her lips, then whispers

into the milky silence:
Make me pure. Forgive.

Teapot

The Little Interior 1926

Hunkered on its haunches,
its conker sheen

is the only colour in the limpid
pallor of her tiny room,

where a curdy light spills
into her china breakfast bowl,

the little glass jar with its cubes
of crystal sugar.

She can feel the gift
of the tea's tepid balm

flow through her veins
conjuring memories

of soda bread cooling on the wire
rack in that dark kitchen,

the Welsh dresser, a pat
of yellow butter in its blue dish,

that home she had to leave
to achieve this lonely state of grace.

Mother

More penitent than bride,
    she stands in her white cotton gown

barefoot below the skylight's
    postage stamp of stars

as if on the banks of the Cledddau.
    In the murky dark she remembers

those Pembroke fields, the damp hedges,
    cattle drovers, the milk cart passing

a broken shed on its way to market.
    The light in the apple orchard.

And then her mother's painful hands
    trying to play Chopin.

Rheumatic gout? Nerves? Exhaustion?
    She never knew–

she just got used to her not being there.
    When, one day, she didn't come home,

she ran around the house chanting
    'Mama's dead. Mama's dead,'

as if a weight had been lifted
    from her small shoulders.

November Afternoon

She no longer knows who she is.
Days flow one into another

in her icy room. Afternoons shorten,
curl back into themselves

dreaming of oranges and heat.
Outside her high window, a tin sky.

Her stove unlit, she cannot rouse
herself to make a fire.

How can she live if every breath
cries for want of love and touch?

Now she must abandon herself
To art. To God.

End these girlish dreams.
Grace is all there is.

Tomorrow she will rise at dawn.
Explore her tiny world

in pigeon-whites and dove-grey,
listen for its fragile heartbeat

beneath the skin of things. Work,
pray, or she'll breakdown
                    and weep.

Angels on the Washing Lines

She hangs her wet stockings
outside the attic window.

Her petticoat and white muslin blouse
to drip-dry between chimney pots

in the first rays of morning sun.
Sweeps the bare floor,

rinses her pink china cup
in the stone sink.

Each act mindful:
a bead, a knot on the rosary

of her days.
Barefoot, she stands, now,

with the poor, watching
her *culottes* billow and dance

in the wind
like angels on the washing line,

teaching her detachment,
obedience, purity.

Girl with a Blue Scarf

She sits against the porridge-coloured wall
watchful, suspicious,
with the look of a frightened fawn.

Her oval face and Slavic eyes wary
beneath the ragged crow-black fringe,
her rodent paws curled

in the mulberry pool of her skirt.
The grate is empty.
The room freezing

for the *carte de charbon* is far too dear.
Both may well ask what they're doing here,
shivering in this pale dun light–

one watchful, the other watching–
the *concierge* from the rue de l'Ouest,
the young painter from Tenby.

Late afternoon.
Her paint is dry as wood ash,
laid down in tiny, speckled strokes

until the girl in a blue scarf
emerges like a thought,
                    like a prayer.

Convalescent

They have changed the white cloth, soaking
out the dark stain with salt. She hardly
remembers days that were different,
filled with the sweet diversions of work.
Time is measured now
in poultices and lint. Below her window
the same hens scratch the same dirt.
Borage and shallots bloom in the herb garden.

Hours stretch faded, formless
and she inhabits the waste lands
behind her eyelids where there is colour,
for her body is white, her limbs thin
as saplings, her hair has lost its walnut sheen.
Once the bodice of this calico dress
clung tight across her apple breasts,
now it hangs like a nun's blue folds.

All morning she sits by the window,
reads, write letters to her cousin.
Outside children's voices shatter
holes in a duck-egg sky. Lilac shadows,
long and dark as a bruise, stretch
across her room. Camphor and crushed
violets fill the throttled air.
On her table, a pink cup and saucer of camomile tea.

From behind drawn blinds sunlight needle-
points the satin gloom. Her skin is grey
as old pastry. In her wicker chair,
with the down cushion plumped to the small
of her back, she dreams of the impossible sun
high over courtyards and dovecot,
illuminating the frailties of small lives,
baking the cracked roofs of barns.

Tiger

When Rodin leaves for Marseille,
she wraps Tiger in a blanket,
heads for Meudon
to camp in a nest of bushes,
and await his return.
Then loses the cat.
Searching among nettles,
rubbish and broken glass,
she snares her skirts on brambles,
sprains her ankle in a muddy hole,
neglects to wash or comb her hair.
Then lays out rows of meat in
a moon-washed garden to tempt
her back. Is mauled by a dog
and left half-naked.
On the cat's return,
thin and full of fleas,
she greets her like a prodigal child.
But when, one midnight,
she produces kittens,
Gwen drowns them in a bucket,
wrapped in newspaper, one by one.

Solitude

...each day she reaches
for the bleached sky
to smear her canvas
in clouds pulverised
with a stone pestle
pigments chalky as
the lime-washed walls
of a nun's cell
or snow's thick fleece
coating the hills of her
Welsh valleys
where lost lambs freeze
in knee-high drifts–
for dead love cannot
heal her now–
only paint and prayer
can offer salvation

Grisaille

Her world is made
of lead and ash.
Grief a force
she cannot control.
Its alchemy
changes everything.
It won't obey her will
but swells like desire
to fill her sleepless nights,
her fretful days,
unmooring her.
In the yawning dark,
her flickering candle
pours its light
into her fathomless sea,
erasing ugliness,
wounds, old battle scars
with the silent
touch of her brush.

Blue

She fills her tiny black notebook
with childish script
on tonalities and techniques:

complimentary of Payn's grey – ombre brûlée
complimentary of Rouge Indienne – vert lac
complimentary of Terre de Sienne – nt. Cassells earth.

Working little by little towards abstraction,
her drawings speak by quiet suggestion,
blocked in, rather than described

with an emphatic line. Experimenting
with darker hues, the little watercolour
she painted one evening in Meudon

flickers with lit windows. A lake
of brilliant blue. Cobalt blue.
That blue you can get lost in.

Chromatic Spectrum

she begins to understand
   that colour is light

imagines waves cleaving
   on the coastline's rugged cliffs

crashing against the rocks
   when only the weak split

or change course   the wavelength
   being the distance

between two corresponding points
   on consecutive waves

it's the same with sunbeams
   red waves remain untouched

as they pass through the atmosphere
   leaving cobalt and violet

scattered in a mesh of molecules
   that make up the sky   so we see blue

but then at sunset   when the air's full
   of dust and salt

agitated vibrations turn the clouds
   Rouge Phénicien

the deep orange of wild geraniums.
   a heavenly red

War

Bombs fall on her beloved Paris.
Crowds jostle in the street terrified
the Germans are coming to eat them.
They will surely die in their beds.

Everywhere *des soldats blessés* stagger
in line, each blind man resting a hand
on the shoulder of the man in front.
Their bandaged eyes frightful with dreams.

The shops are shut. There's nothing to sell.
Everyone's hungry. Fuel must be gathered
from the *bois*. An alien, now, England
is a foreign land. To busy herself,

she borrows books from the library.
Interprets for American soldiers,
speaks English to the wounded.
For all is ruin, the colour of cruelty.

Brittany

It's the Manoir de Vauxclair that now holds her heart,
forlorn in its neglected garden. The tall iron gates,
painted cornflower blue, leading to a leafy lane,

the meadow with a stream. Oxeye daisies. Cat's ear.
Sweet Vernal. When the farmer gives her the key,
she finds moulded ceilings, soot-filled stoves,

porcelain tiles painted with blue doves. A salon
where strained sunlight pours through a mesh
of creepers outside the tall windows casting

a green net on the red brick floor. She loves the quiet.
The pious silence. Though the gossips in Pléneuf try
to catch a glimpse of *la femme Anglaise*

all dressed in black, living alone with her cats
that give birth in the empty *salle à manger,*
leave gizzards of murdered mice beneath her bed.

Mornings she walks to the beach at Grève des Vallées.
Counts waves like rosary beads: ten small ones,
then a lucky swell. Learning to be alone. Work.

God's Little Artist

She yearns to be a saint.
A child of God.

For her work to have
the serenity of prayer.

Her God is a God of quietness,
so she must be quiet.

His love is constant.
It does not despise,

or rebuff like carnal love.
She would live without

a body, now. Its fleshy needs,
its urgent desires,

yet cannot pray for long.
Between her sewing threads,

her rosary lies broken,
wooden beads scattered

among old buttons,
Her barren room

washed luminous
with light.

Lead White

She prepares the canvases
herself. Develops a numerical
system for tonal values.
Abandons traditional glazes
for impasto applied in small
dabs with a stubby brush
that make the surfaces shimmer
like Byzantine mosaics.
Augustus is astonished.
Says he's ready to shut up shop.
But this whiteness will kill her.
The shades from eggshells
and oysters, the burned bones
of lambs are too gritty and grey.
What she needs is lustre,
so chooses the cruellest
with a heart of black.
Then dismisses the lethargy,
the deathly pallor,
the blue tinge around
her gums, the little marks
circling her wrists:
this slow dying for her art.

Dieppe

She won't see a doctor. Can hardly stand.
Shuffles her bed into the garden shed
used as a studio so she can see the stars,
though it's open to the wind and rain.

Now Poland has fallen she can't face
another war in France, longs to return
to the Preseli hills, the Gwaun, Syfynwy
and Taf. When she climbs from

the train carrying no luggage,
she exudes a stench of poverty.
Collapses. Crowds gather and gawp.
Assume she's a derelict, take her

to the local hospice to die.
Augustus promises a headstone but,
somehow, it slips his mind. No matter,
when she's been so fearless. So true:
                                    herself.

Notes

1. 'Slade': Henry Tonks, 1862-1937. A British surgeon and, later, draughtsman and painter who became an influential teacher at the Slade School of Fine Art.

2. 'Love is Lonelier than Solitude': Gwen had a series of cats. Tiger was one of them. Rose Beuret was a French seamstress, one of Rodin's muses, who lived with him for 53 years, marrying him just weeks before her death in 1917.

3. 'Fire'. The term Red Indian was the phrase in use at the time, but is unacceptable now. Native Americans or First People is more appropriate.

4. 'Convalescent'. A version of this poem written in the first person appeared in my first collection *Everything Begins with the Skin* (Enitharmon)

Acknowledgements

Thanks are due to the poet and sculptor Stephen Duncan, and to Moniza Alvi for their close and attentive reading of these poems. Also to Bernedette Cremin and Rosie Jackson for their helpful suggestions and the editors at Seren. Susan Chitty's biography *Gwen John 1876-1939* was invaluable in my research.

Author

Sue Hubbard is an award-winning poet, novelist and art critic. She has published five collections of poetry, most recently *Radium Dreams* (Women's Art Collection, Murray Edwards College, Cambridge), which is a collaboration with the artist Eileen Cooper RA, inspired by the remarkable life of Marie Curie. Sue has also published three novels with her fourth, *Flatlands*, forthcoming from Pushkin Press in June 2023. Sue's poems have been read on Radio 3, Radio 4 and RTE, and appeared in *The Irish Times*, *The London Magazine* and *Acumen*, as well as prestigious anthologies. As an art critic she has written for *Time Out*, *The Independent*, *The New Statesman* and *The London Magazine* and is a senior writer for *Artlyst*. A collection of her art writings *Adventures in Art* was published by Damien Hirst's Other Criteria.